AF228564

Tiger Cubs

Julie Murray

abdobooks.com

Published by Abdo Kids, a division of ABDO, P.O. Box 398166, Minneapolis, Minnesota 55439.
Copyright © 2019 by Abdo Consulting Group, Inc. International copyrights reserved in all countries.
No part of this book may be reproduced in any form without written permission from the publisher.
Abdo Kids Junior™ is a trademark and logo of Abdo Kids.

Printed in the United States of America, North Mankato, Minnesota.

102018

012019

THIS BOOK CONTAINS
RECYCLED MATERIALS

Photo Credits: Alamy, iStock, Minden Pictures, Shutterstock, ©Gerard Lacz/Shutterstock p23

Production Contributors: Teddy Borth, Jennie Forsberg, Grace Hansen

Design Contributors: Christina Doffing, Candice Keimig, Dorothy Toth

Library of Congress Control Number: 2018946191

Publisher's Cataloging-in-Publication Data

Names: Murray, Julie, author.

Title: Tiger cubs / by Julie Murray.

Description: Minneapolis, Minnesota : Abdo Kids, 2019 | Series: Baby animals set 2 |
    Includes glossary, index and online resources (page 24).

Identifiers: ISBN 9781532181689 (lib. bdg.) | ISBN 9781532182662 (ebook) |
    ISBN 9781532183157 (Read-to-me ebook)

Subjects: LCSH: Tiger cubs--Juvenile literature. | Baby animals--Juvenile literature. |
    Zoo animals--Infancy--Juvenile literature. | Tigers--Juvenile literature.

Classification: DDC 599.756--dc2

Table of Contents

Tiger Cubs

A **female** tiger has 2 to 4 cubs at a time.

Cubs are small. They can weigh 3 pounds (1.4 kg) at birth.

They are born with fur
and stripes.

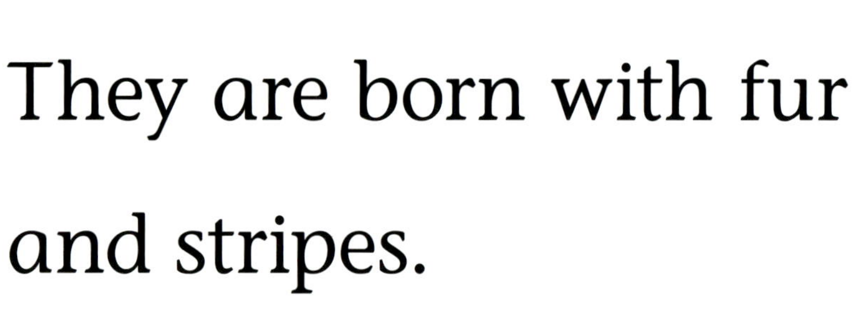

They stay in the **den**.

This keeps them safe.

They drink their mother's milk.

Soon they will eat meat too.

12

13

The mother licks her cubs.

She keeps them clean.

The cubs are 6 weeks old.

They come out of the **den**.

They learn to hunt. They watch
their mom.

The cubs love to play.

Watch a Tiger Cub Grow!

newborn

2 months

18 months

36 months

Glossary

den
the resting place of some animals.

female
a girl animal that can have young.

Index

Visit **abdokids.com** and use this code to access crafts, games, videos, and more!